MW00981865

Endorsements

"In a complex and changing world, simplicity is so refreshing. Simple Praise is exactly that; a powerful collection of faith filled statements about who God is. This book contains so many valuable prayers and words of praise that will build faith in anyone who will read it. Whether you have served God for a lifetime, or are still wondering if He is real, this book will be an encouragement to you and give practical words to express the thoughts of your heart."

– Jay Smith
Senior Pastor, Cedar Park Church, Bothell, Washington

"This book of love, encouragement and wisdom belongs beside my Bible in all my journeys with the Holy Spirit."

– Marion F. Henny
Chairman of the Board of Whidbey Telecom

SIMPLE PRAISE

The secret to weathering life's storms

Praise God the Three-In-One

Mercy Dworzak

WestBow Press books may be ordered through booksellers or by contacting:

WestBow Press
A Division of Thomas Nelson & Zondervan
1663 Liberty Drive
Bloomington, IN 47403
www.westbowpress.com
1 (866) 928-1240

ISBN: 978-1-9736-2730-2 (sc)
ISBN: 978-1-9736-3248-1 (hc)
ISBN: 978-1-9736-2729-6 (e)

Print information available on the last page.

WestBow Press rev. date: 07/30/2018

Dedication

To my beloved mother, now in glory, who modeled for me steadfast faith in our Lord Jesus Christ, and love for all people.

Contents

SECTION 5: COMMITMENT

Introduction

It takes faith to worship God. When we praise and thank God, we acknowledge that God exists and that He rewards us for trusting in him. Faith honors God. God is FAITHFUL to honor our faith. We praise God for WHO HE IS and thank God for WHAT HE HAS DONE.

Our entire life is worship – what we do with our life and how we do it demonstrates what and whom we worship. **We live out, with all our strength, what we really believe and love with all our heart, soul and mind.** That is why Jesus said in Matthew 22:37, "Love the Lord your God with all your heart, with all your soul and with all your mind." This is worship!

Praise is an expression of our faith in God and it is an important way to worship God. Praising God prospers our soul. We cannot give God anything without receiving manifold blessings in return. It is not that we "have to" give God praise but WHO GOD IS warrants our praise and worship. We can praise God alone or in a congregation of believers. Both are necessary!

Thanksgiving is also an expression of our faith in God. When we give thanks, we acknowledge God as the source of all the good things we have come to possess and accomplish. **Being grateful helps us more than anything else because gratitude renews our mind and brings healing to our soul and body**

This book is comprised of short sentences to give praise to our HOLY GOD and to thank him for the marvelous deeds He has done. These are words of kings, prophets, judges, disciples, apostles, and followers of Jesus Christ found in the Holy Bible.

May you be blessed as you fill God's throne room with your praise and thanksgiving.

Section 1

Praise the Father

Father Loves

God is the Creator of the heavens and the earth, the author of all life, and has no beginning or end.

This all-knowing God knew, before He created man, that He must sacrifice Jesus His Son, to purchase man back from the kingdom of darkness that would enslave. He knew that He must send the Holy Spirit to guide man through his earthly journey, and lead man to his eternal home. Despite the cost of the sacrifice required to redeem man, God said, “Let us make man” Genesis 1:26. This is the Father heart of God!

Love Gives!

Father God longs for his children to come home to him.

No matter how young or old you are, you have a Father in heaven. He is the Ancient of Days. He is watching over you every moment of the day, caring for all your needs, and waiting for you to run into his arms for strength and comfort.

In the next few pages you can read about and praise this awesome God, our Father.

Father I Honor You

God, the blessed and only Ruler, the King of Kings and Lord of Lords, who alone is immortal and who lives in unapproachable light, whom no one has seen or can see. To him be honor and might forever. Amen.

1 Timothy 6:15b – 16

Father You Are Awesome

Father you are God Most High.

Father you are Creator of everything.

Father you are Majesty in Heaven.

Father you are King of all the earth.

Father you have no beginning or end of life.

Father you are God of Divine nature.

Father you are Almighty.

Father you are Holy and True.

Father you are Eternal.

Father you are Ancient of Days.

Father you are the Majestic Glory.

Father you are the God of Peace.

Father you are the Everlasting One.

Father you are Kind.

Father you are Tolerant.

Father you are Longsuffering.

Father You Are Awesome

Father you are full of Compassion.

Father you are Merciful.

Father you are Forgiving.

Father you are Patient.

Father you are Slow to Anger.

Father you are Faithful.

Father you are Just.

Father you are Love.

Father you are Gracious.

Father you are consuming Fire.

Father you are the Mighty Warrior.

Father you are Invincible.

Father you are Great, and your Hand is strong.

Father you are Mighty and firm in your Purpose.

Father you are the God of Order.

Father You Are Awesome

Father you are the God of our spirit.

Father you are Greater than any mortal.

Father you do not let mortals prevail against you.

Father you are not a human being to change your mind.

Father you are not human, so you don't lie.

Father you are not slow in keeping your promises.

Father you are the Light and in you there is no evil at all.

Father you are the Righteous Judge.

Father you are the zealous God.

Father you are the Builder of everything.

Father you are Strong.

Father you are a Rock of Refuge.

Father you are a mighty Fortress.

Father you are the God of glorious riches.

Father your word is Right and True.

Father I Worship You

"Great and marvelous are your deeds, Lord God Almighty.
Just and true are your ways,
King of the nations.
Who will not fear you, Lord,
and bring glory to your name?
For you alone are holy.
All nations will come
and worship before you,
for your righteous acts have been revealed."

Revelation 15:3b-4

Father You Are Awesome

Father your voice is majestic.

Father your voice is like the sound of rushing water.

Father your voice is powerful.

Father your voice shakes the desert.

Father your voice twists the oaks and strips the forests bare.

Father your voice strikes with flashes of lightning.

Father your right hand shatters the enemy.

Father you are greatly to be feared.

Father your works are Awesome and Mighty.

Father you are the King of Heaven.

Father you are God in heaven above and on the earth below.

Father you are God of invisible qualities.

Father you are Spirit.

Father you are OMNIPOTENT.

Father you are OMNIPRESENT.

Father you are OMNICIENT.

Father your voice is a wisper

Father You Alone Are God

LORD Almighty, the God of Israel, enthroned between the cherubim, you alone are God over all the kingdoms of the earth. You made the heaven and earth.

Isaiah 37:16

Father You Are Awesome

Father you are exalted in your Power.

Father you are worthy of all Glory.

Father you are Sovereign over all the kingdoms on the earth.

Father you are Immutable.

Father your Name is Holy.

Father your Name is Great and Awesome.

Father your Name is Jehovah Jireh – our Provider.

Father your Name is Jehovah Shalom – our Peace.

Father your Name is Jehovah Rapha – our Healer.

Father your Name is Jehovah Sabaoth – Lord of Hosts.

Father you are seated on your holy throne.

Father you are clothed with splendor and majesty.

Father you are forever praised and adored.

Father you are enthroned as the Holy One.

Father your kingdom is an eternal kingdom.

Father your dominion endures throughout all generations.

Father There Is None Like You

Who is like you, LORD God Almighty? You, LORD, are mighty, and your faithfulness surrounds you.

Psalm 89:8

Father You Are Awesome

Father your years will never end.

Father you reign for ever and ever.

Father you are AMAZING.

Father you are AWESOME.

Father you are WONDERFUL.

Father you are MARVELOUS.

Father you are The GREAT I AM.

Praise Notes

Section 2

Praise Jesus the Son

Jesus Saves

God made man in his image and had constant fellowship with him in the garden of Eden. But when man sinned by disobeying God, man's spirit died and he was separated from God. As there is no way man can earn forgiveness for his sins by any works he can do on this earth, God, who is Holy and Righteous, himself made a way.

At the appointed time, God the Father sent his word to become flesh. The only begotten Son of God, Jesus, became the Son of man. God who is holy, cannot let sin go unpunished. Therefore, he placed the sins of all mankind, past, present and future, upon Jesus as he hung on the cross. Through Jesus Christ, God reconciled all men to himself.

Jesus came into the world to save us sinners and to restore our relationship to our Father. Jesus chose to endure the ridicule and the cruel death at the hands of men rather than to live without mankind for all eternity.

Jesus is our Savior, Redeemer, Friend and much more. In the next few pages you will be blessed to learn all that he is, and can be, in your life.

Jesus I Give You Glory

Worthy is the Lamb,
who was slain, to receive power and
wealth, and wisdom and strength
and honor and glory
and praise!

Revelation 5:12b

Jesus You Are Awesome

Jesus you are the Son of God Most High.

Jesus you are God who WAS and IS and who IS to Come.

Jesus you are the Bright and Morning Star.

Jesus you are the Faithful and the True Witness from God.

Jesus you are the Ruler of all Creation.

Jesus you are the Image of the Invisible God.

Jesus you are the exact Representation of God the Father.

Jesus you are the Firstborn over all Creation.

Jesus you are the Heir of all things.

Jesus you are the Sustainer who holds all things together.

Jesus you are far Above all rule and authority.

Jesus you are Seated at the right hand of the Father in Heaven.

Jesus you have Sovereignty over everything.

Jesus you are the Treasure House of Wisdom.

Jesus you are the Source of all Knowledge.

Jesus you are the Word that created all things.

Jesus you are Head over all power.

Jesus You Are Awesome

Jesus your Name is far Above every name.

Jesus your Wisdom is great and awesome.

Jesus your Purposes are eternal.

Jesus your Dominion is an everlasting dominion.

Jesus you Rule over the nations.

Jesus you are the Righteous One.

Jesus you are the Great God.

Jesus you are the WORD of God.

Jesus you are the WORD of Life.

Jesus you are the King of the Ages.

Jesus you are the Only Begotten Son of God.

Jesus you are the Seed of the Woman.

Jesus you are the Wisdom of God.

Jesus you are the Lord of the Sabbath.

Jesus you are the Lion of Judah.

Jesus you are the Great High Priest forever.

JESUS YOU ARE AWESOME

Jesus you are the Chief Cornerstone.

Jesus you are the Faithful Scribe.

Jesus you are the Stone the builders rejected.

Jesus you are the Root of Jesse.

Jesus you are the Son of David.

Jesus you are the Messiah.

Jesus you are the Christ.

Jesus you are the Anointed One.

Jesus you are LORD.

Jesus you are Gracious.

Jesus you are Humble.

Jesus you are Good.

Jesus you are the Redeemer.

Jesus you are the Beloved Son of God.

Jesus you are the Prince and Savior at the right hand of God.

Jesus you are the Author of Salvation.

Jesus I Give You Praise

"To him who sits on the throne and to the Lamb be praise and honor and glory and power, for ever and ever!"

Revelation 5:13b

Jesus You Are Awesome

Jesus you are the Word made Flesh.

Jesus you are the Lamb Without Blemish.

Jesus you are the Passover Lamb.

Jesus you are the Power of God for Salvation.

Jesus you are the Bread of Life from Heaven.

Jesus you are the Atoning sacrifice.

Jesus you are the Fragrant Offering to God.

Jesus you are Holy, Blameless and Pure.

Jesus you are Mighty to Save.

Jesus you are the Savior of the world.

Jesus you are the Risen Lord.

Jesus you are Alive Forevermore.

Jesus your Love surpasses all knowledge.

Jesus your Blood speaks forgiveness.

Jesus your Gospel is the Word of Truth.

Jesus you are the Light of the world.

Jesus you are the Spring of Living Water.

Jesus You Are Awesome

Jesus you are much Superior to the Angels.

Jesus you are Head over all things of the church.

Jesus you are Glorified through the church.

Jesus you are the Builder of broken lives.

Jesus you are the Bearer of our burdens.

Jesus you are the Deliverer.

Jesus you are the Door.

Jesus you are the Way.

Jesus you are the Truth.

Jesus you are the Life.

Jesus you are the Justifier.

Jesus you are the Last Adam.

Jesus you are the Intercessor.

Jesus you are the Rebuilder of broken walls.

Jesus you are the Restorer of the lost.

Jesus you are the Mediator of the New Covenant.

Jesus You Are Awesome

Jesus you are the Captain of Our Salvation.

Jesus you are the Great Advocate between God and Man.

Jesus you are the Chief Shepherd.

Jesus you are the Great Physician.

Jesus you are the Same yesterday, today and forever.

Jesus you are the True Vine.

Jesus you are the Author and Finisher of our faith.

Jesus you are the Author of Life.

Jesus you are the Baptizer in the Holy Spirit.

Jesus you are the Everlasting Father.

Jesus you are the Prince of Peace.

Jesus you are the Wonderful Counselor.

Jesus you are the Mighty God.

Jesus you are the Living One.

Jesus you are the Immortal One.

Jesus you are God of Grace and Truth.

Jesus You Are Awesome

Jesus you are the Manna from Heaven.

Jesus you are the Living Stone.

Jesus you are the Mighty Tower.

Jesus you are the Precious Cornerstone

Jesus you are the Prophet of the Lord.

Jesus you are the Rock of Salvation.

Jesus you are the Mighty Warrior of God.

Jesus you are the Protector.

Jesus you are the Stronghold in trouble.

Jesus you are the Judge and the Lawgiver.

Jesus you are the Gift from heaven beyond description.

Jesus you are the Firstborn from the Dead.

Jesus you are the Resurrection and the Life.

Jesus you are the Dayspring from on High.

Jesus you are the Friend.

Jesus you are the Kinsman Redeemer.

Jesus You Are Awesome

Jesus you are the Faithful Lover.

Jesus you are the Heavenly Bridegroom.

Jesus you are the Fairest of ten thousand.

Jesus you are the Rose of Sharon.

Jesus you are the Lily of the Valley.

Jesus you are All together lovely.

Jesus you are my Song.

Jesus you are the Lover of my soul.

Jesus you are the Hope of Glory.

Jesus you are the Victorious one.

Jesus you are God who Ascended to Heaven.

Jesus you are worshipped by all God's angels.

Jesus you are Exalted to the Highest place.

Jesus you are Crowned with glory and honor.

Jesus you are the Alpha and Omega.

Jesus you are the Beginning and the End.

Jesus I Adore You

Now to the King eternal, immortal, invisible, the only God, be honor and glory for ever and ever. Amen

1 Timothy 1:17

Jesus You Are Awesome

Jesus you are the First and the Last.

Jesus you are the God "I Am".

Jesus you are the soon and coming King.

Jesus you are the Lord of Glory.

Jesus you are the King of Kings.

Jesus you are GOD.

Praise Notes

Section 3

Praise the Holy Spirit

Holy Spirit Helps

Holy Spirit is Jesus in us. When Jesus was on the earth, his presence was limited by location. Jesus said that it would be beneficial for us that He would leave the earth and ascend to heaven. Because then the Father would send the Holy Spirit to come and dwell inside of us.

Jesus had to shed his blood for the cleansing of our sins, so the Holy Spirit can come and live inside of us. Before Jesus, the blood of goats and bulls sacrificed as sin offerings could only cover the sins of the people.

But the blood of Jesus removes our sins and makes us holy, so we can receive the gift of the Holy Spirit.

God the Father pours out his Spirit on those who ask him. So ask and you will receive.

In the next few pages you can come to know and praise the Holy Spirit who is our helper and much more.

Holy Spirit Live In Me

And I will ask the Father, and he will give you another advocate to help and be with you forever – the Spirit of truth. The world cannot accept him, because it neither sees him nor knows him. But you know him, for he lives with you and will be in you.

John 14:16-17

Holy Spirit You Are Awesome

Holy Spirit you are the Comforter.

Holy Spirit you are the Helper.

Holy Spirit you are the Guide.

Holy Spirit you are the Teacher.

Holy Spirit you are the Counselor.

Holy Spirit you are the Advocate.

Holy Spirit you are the unsurpassed Wisdom of God.

Holy Spirit you are the unfailing Love of God.

Holy Spirit you are the incomparable Power of God.

Holy Spirit you are the Seal of ownership.

Holy Spirit you are the Guarantee of the heavenly inheritance.

Holy Spirit you are the Foretaste of future glory.

Holy Spirit you are the Presence and the Power of God in us.

Holy Spirit you know the Mind of God.

Holy Spirit you bring Revelation from heaven.

Holy Spirit you give us God's Life.

Holy Spirit Work In Me

But the Advocate, the Holy Spirit, whom the Father will send in my name, will teach you all things and will remind you of everything I have said to you.

John 14:26

Holy Spirit You Are Awesome

Holy Spirit you bring us God's Mercy.

Holy Spirit you are the Spirit of Truth.

Holy Spirit you remind God's truth to us.

Holy Spirit you sanctify us.

Holy Spirit you destroy the yoke of burden.

Holy Spirit you help us overcome sinful cravings.

Holy Spirit you break the chains of bondage.

Holy Spirit you help us worship God.

Holy Spirit you pray through us.

Holy Spirit you speak through us.

Holy Spirit you enlighten our minds.

Holy Spirit you renew our minds.

Holy Spirit you lead us into all truth.

Holy Spirit you live inside of us.

Holy Spirit you fill us with joy.

Holy Spirit you fill us with love.

Holy Spirit Live Through Me

God has raised this Jesus to Life, and we are all witnesses of it. Exalted to the right hand of God, he has received from the Father the promised Holy Spirit and has poured out what you now see and hear.

Acts 2:32-33

Holy Spirit You Are Awesome

Holy Spirit you give strength and power to our inner man.

Holy Spirit you fill us with confident hope.

Holy Spirit you give us holy boldness.

Holy Spirit you give us the power to be a witness.

Holy Spirit you bring to remembrance the words of Jesus.

Holy Spirit you instruct us the way God has chosen for us.

Holy Spirit you empower us to stand strong in faith.

Holy Spirit you are the Gift of God to us.

Praise Notes

Section 4

Give Thanks

I Give You Thanks

Give thanks in all circumstances; for this is God's will for you in Christ Jesus.

1 Thessalonians 5:18

Praise the LORD, my soul, and forget not all his benefits – who forgives all your sins and heals all your diseases, who redeems your life from the pit and crowns you with love and compassion, who satisfies your desires with good things so that your youth is renewed like the eagle's.

Psalm 103:2-5

Giving thanks is an expression of a grateful heart. When we focus our minds on things that we can be thankful for, we develop faith in God. Faith supplants fear and anxiety.

Practicing gratitude changes our attitude. Our attitude causes us to rise or fall in life. A positive attitude is attractive, and helps us succeed. With God's help, we can become grateful people.

This section highlights some things for which we owe God gratitude.

SALVATION
PROVISION
DELIVERANCE
PROTECTION
REFUGE
HELP
COMFORT
HEALING
PURPOSE
GUIDANCE
ABUNDANT LIFE
REWARDS
HEAVEN

You Are My Savior

Thank You for Salvation

Your Sacrifice Is Sufficient

We all, like sheep, have gone astray, each of us has turned to our own way; and the LORD has laid on him the iniquity of us all. He was oppressed and afflicted, yet he did not open his mouth; he was led like a lamb to the slaughter, and as sheep before its shearers is silent, so he did not open his mouth.

Isaiah 53:6-7

How much more, then, will the blood of Christ, who through the eternal Spirit offered himself unblemished to God, cleanse our conscience from acts that lead to death, so that we may serve the living God!

Hebrews 9:14

Thank You for Salvation

Father, you so loved the whole world you sent Jesus.

You did not send Jesus to condemn the world.

You did not send Jesus to judge the world.

You sent Jesus to seek and save the lost.

Jesus, you came into the world to save sinners.

You came to rescue the perishing.

You humbled yourself and became a man.

You were not ashamed to be called my God.

You chose me before the creation of the world.

You died so I can have eternal life.

You died for me while I was still a sinner.

You died as a ransom to set me free.

You tasted death on my behalf.

You destroyed the power of death over me.

You rescued me from the kingdom of darkness.

You saved me from the hand of the enemy who wants to destroy me.

Your Salvation Is A Gift

For the wages of sin is death, but the gift of God is eternal life in Christ Jesus our Lord.

Romans 6:23

But the gift is not like the trespass. For if the many died by the trespass of the one man, how much more did God's grace and the gift that came by the grace of the one man, Jesus Christ, overflow to the many!

Romans 5:15

Thank You for Salvation

You did not count my sins against me.

You bore my sins on your body on the tree.

You nailed to the cross everything that condemned me.

You offered yourself as a sacrifice to God.

You provided purification for my sins.

Your precious blood justified me.

You redeemed me from being a slave to sin.

You forgave all my sins.

You rescued me from judgment and hell fire.

You brought me into Your eternal kingdom.

You reconciled me with my Heavenly Father.

You made me a new creation.

You made me a child of God.

You lavished on me the gift of righteousness.

You gave me access to the holy presence of God.

You saved me not because of what I have done.

Your Grace Is Amazing

Like the rest, we were by nature deserving of wrath. But because of his great love for us, God, who is rich in mercy, made us alive with Christ even when we were dead in transgressions – it is by grace you have been saved.

Ephesians 2:3b-5

Thank You for Salvation

You saved me because of your mercy and love.

Your obedience has made me righteous.

Your resurrection has given me hope.

You are the door to the Father in heaven.

Your salvation is for me and my household.

You are the WAY, the TRUTH, and the LIFE.

Jesus there is no other name but your name that saves.

You are my SAVIOR!

You Are My Provider

Thank You for Provision

Your Provision Is Plentiful

Therefore, I tell you, do not worry about your life, what you will eat or drink; or about your body, what you will wear... Look at the birds of the air; they do not sow or reap or store away in barns, and yet your heavenly Father, feeds them. Are you not much more valuable than they?
But seek first his kingdom and his righteousness, and all these things will be given to you as well.

Matthew 6:25-26, 33

Thank You For Provision

You provide for the just and the unjust.

You provide abundantly.

You send rain to the earth.

You provide grass for the cattle.

You care for birds of the air.

You tell me I am valuable.

You provide for all my needs.

You load me with benefits every day.

You give me every good and perfect gift.

You sustain me by your power.

You care about all my problems.

You help me in my time of need.

You listen to all my prayers.

You answer me from your holy throne.

You use the wrong anyone does to me for good.

You do what is just and right for me.

Your Resource is Unlimited

And my God will meet all your needs according to the riches of his glory in Christ Jesus.

Philippians 4:19

The LORD is my shepherd, I lack nothing. He makes me lie down in green pastures, he leads me beside quiet water, he refreshes my soul.

Psalm 23:1-2

Thank You For Provision

You help me through the difficulty.

You help me when I am powerless.

You spare me from sorrow.

You lift me when I fall.

You help me not be overwhelmed by worldly worries.

You remove my grieving clothes and clothe me with joy.

You turn my problems into opportunities.

You make a way in the wilderness for me.

You make streams to flow in the desert for me.

You do what is impossible for me to do.

You are my Shepherd taking care of all my needs.

You are with me wherever I go.

You give me the ability to tackle everything that comes my way.

You make me stand in confidence and strength.

You help me make the best of everything I have.

You have not forsaken me and you never will.

Your Supply is Bountiful

He has shown kindness by giving you rain from heaven and crops in their seasons; he provides you with plenty of food and fills your heart with joy.

Acts 14:17b

He grants peace to your borders and satisfies you with the finest of wheat.

Psalm 147:14

Thank You For Provision

You help me be successful at work.

You help me accomplish the task set before me.

You help me to be focused and disciplined.

You reward me for working diligently.

You give me riches and restore my fortune.

You give me power to enjoy wealth.

You deal bountifully with me.

You prosper the work of my hands.

You help me stand strong in faith.

You take care of all my tomorrows.

You fill my heart with joy that nothing can take away.

You give me peace when I lie down to rest.

You strengthen my heart.

You are my rising sun.

You turn your face towards me.

You make my face radiant.

Your Faithfulness Is Everlasting

For I have always been mindful of your unfailing love and have lived in reliance on your faithfulness.

Psalm 26:3

Your love, LORD, reaches to the heavens, your **faithfulness** to the skies.

Psalm 36:5

Thank You For Provision

You give me a happy heart.

You call me beautiful.

You love me with unfailing love.

You are forever faithful.

You are my PROVIDER!

Praise Notes

Thank You for Deliverance

You Are My Deliverer

It is because of God's protection that the devil is unable to snuff the life out of us. The devil has no authority over our lives when we are surrendered to God and are under God's Sovereign rule.

God cannot be tempted with evil nor does He tempt anyone with evil. There is no evil in God. The devil however influences our thoughts and imaginations, and tempts us continuously. When we fall into temptation we give a foothold to the evil one.

In 1 Peter 5:8 we read,

"Be alert and of sober mind.

Your enemy the devil prowls around like a roaring lion

looking for someone to devour."

The devil is throwing his arrows to attack us, spreading his snare to trap us, and hunting us down to rob us of our destiny and to mar the image of God in us. But God who is in us is greater than the evil one in the world. God is faithful to come to our rescue and deliver us from the evil one. All we need to do is to call on Him.

He is our rescue!

Your Deliverance Is Astounding

He got up, rebuked the wind and said to the waves, "Quiet! Be still!" Then the wind died down and it was completely calm.

Mark 4:39

When they came to Jesus, they saw the man who had been possessed by the legion of demons, sitting there, dressed and in his right mind; and they were afraid.

Mark 5:15

Thank You For Deliverance

You hear my cry for help.

You come to my rescue quickly.

You hear my cry for mercy.

You lift me out of the depths.

You deliver me from depression.

You deliver me from despondency.

You deliver me from my suffering.

You save me out of all my troubles.

You do not let me be put to shame.

You free me from my distress.

You destroy the chains that bind me.

You give relief from my misery.

You destroy the yoke of burden over me.

You defend me against the evil one.

You calm the storm in my life.

You set me free from fear and doubt.

Your Might is Boundless

Jesus speaking of himself says in Luke 4:18 The Spirit of the Lord is on me, because he has anointed me to proclaim good news to the poor. He has sent me to proclaim freedom for the prisoners and recovery of sight for the blind, to set the oppressed free.

Thank You For Deliverance

You deliver me from the power of the evil one.

You help me destroy the strongholds in my thoughts and imaginations.

You break the power of addiction over me.

You help me escape the trickery of the enemy.

You foil the plans of the enemy against me.

You hinder the strategies of the enemy against me.

You alert me of the deception of the enemy.

You expose the lies the enemy puts in my mind.

You do not let the will of the enemy prevail against me.

You do not let the enemy triumph over me.

You spare me from going down into the pit.

You deliver me from the hands of evil doers.

You deliver me from the deceitful and the unjust.

You deliver me from abuse and insults.

You bring about justice when I call out to you.

You deliver me to serve you.

Your Power Is Unrestrained

The Lord, the God of battle, has spoken – who can change his plans? When his hand moves, who can stop him?

Isaiah 14:27 Living Bible (TLB)

Thank You For Deliverance

You act on my behalf as I wait on You.

You rescue me from the hand of my oppressors.

You do not turn me over to the desire of my foes.

You shut the mouth of the lions for me.

You uphold my right and my cause.

You vindicate me by your power.

You let no weapon formed against me to prosper.

You cause authorities to show me favor.

You cause leaders to have compassion on me.

You deliver me by your powerful hand.

You deliver me because of your compassion.

You delight me with your deliverance.

You surround me with songs of joy.

You are the horn of my salvation.

You are the savior of the world.

You are the deliverer of the needy.

Your Strength is Awesome

There is no one like...God...who rides across the heavens to help you and on the clouds in his majesty.

Deuteronomy 33:26

THANK YOU FOR DELIVERANCE

You are the rescuer of the weak.

Your Name is Great.

Your Hand is Mighty.

Your arms are outstretched.

You are my DELIVERER!

You Are My Protector

Thank You for Protection

Your Shelter Is Secure

He will cover you with his feathers, and under his wings you will find refuge; his faithfulness will be your shield and rampart.

Psalm 91:4

But the Lord is faithful, and he will strengthen you and **protect** you from the evil one.

2 Thessalonians 3:3

Thank You For Protection

You guard my life.

You watch over me.

You protect me from harm.

You are a shield around me.

You are the stronghold of my life.

You are greater than the one in the world.

You protect me from people with bad intentions.

You preserve me from the dread of the enemy.

You guard my steps from the trap of the evil one.

You shield me from the arrows of the evil one.

You raise up a standard against the enemy that seeks to destroy me.

You make the enemy turn back.

You protect me from ways devised to trip me.

You protect me from the lash of the tongue.

You protect me from those who malign me.

You know the anxious thoughts of my heart.

Your Mercy Is Unending

Jesus' prayer in John 17:11, 17:15

I will remain in the world no longer, but they are still in the world, and I am coming to you. Holy Father, **protect** them by the power of your name, the name you gave me, so that they may be one as we are one.
My prayer is not that you take them out of the world but that you **protect** them from the evil one.

Thank You For Protection

You keep me safe from the hands of the wicked.

You protect me when I call on your name.

You give me wisdom that preserves me.

You give me discretion that protects me.

You give me understanding that guards me.

You hold me by your hand and defend me.

You hide me under the shadow of your wings.

You shelter me by your presence.

You order my steps and guard my course.

You bless my going out and coming in.

You help me dwell in safety.

You keep me as the apple of your eye.

You give your angels to guard me.

You place a hedge of protection around me.

Your eyes are always on me.

Your love and faithfulness protect me.

Your Protection Is Sure

You are my hiding place; you will protect me from trouble and surround me with songs of deliverance.

Psalm 32:7

"Because he loves me," says the Lord, "I will rescue him; I will protect him, for he acknowledges my name.

Psalm 91:14

Thank You For Protection

You guard my heart and soul.

You are my guardian-redeemer.

You are my rear guard.

You are my hiding place.

You are my PROTECTOR!

Praise Notes

Thank You for Refuge

You are my Refuge

God allows trials in our lives to test our faith in Him, our commitment to Him, and to purify us like a goldsmith refines gold. But we can run into His Everlasting arms, find refuge, and receive strength to endure the trial. God will provide a way for us to keep standing on our feet during the trial and will **lead us out of it with greater power than ever before.** We read in 1 Corinthians 10:13,

"No temptation has overtaken you except what is common to mankind. And God is faithful; he will not let you be tempted beyond what you can bear. But when you are tempted, he will also provide a way out so that you can endure it."

Trials and testing can come as afflictions or temptations from the devil. For the righteous man, Job, it was affliction. For the Righteous One, Jesus, it was temptation. Jesus was led by the Spirit into the wilderness to be tempted by the devil only to return with more power to minister. When we go through a time of trial and testing, our recourse is to put on the full armor of God and to take refuge in Him. The purpose behind trial and testing is to develop the image of Jesus in us. God is committed to helping us be victorious.

Let us continue to express our trust in Him and rely on His goodness and infinite love.

Your Armor Is Mighty

The weapons we fight with are not the weapons of the world. On the contrary, they have divine power to demolish strongholds.

2 Corinthians 6:7

Put on the full armor of God, so that you can take a stand against the devil's schemes. For our struggle is not against flesh and blood, but against the rulers, against the authorities, against the powers of this dark world and against spiritual forces of evil in the heavenly realms. Therefore put on the full armor of God, so that when the day of evil comes, you may be able to stand your ground, and after you have done everything, to stand.

Ephesians 6:11-13

Thank You For Refuge

You have given me the full armor of God.

Your armor is mighty to pulling down strongholds of the devil.

You have given me SALVATION as my **helmet**.

Your salvation protects my mind from the influence of the evil one.

You have given me FATIH as my **shield**.

You have given me the power to extinguish the flaming arrows of the evil one through faith in you.

You have given me the power to overcome the world through faith in you.

You have given me your RIGHTEOUSNESS as my **breastplate**.

Your righteousness protects my heart from evil desires.

You have given me the TRUTH, as my **belt**.

Your Word trains me in righteousness and guards my steps.

You have given me your SPIRIT and your WORD as my **sword**.

Your Holy Spirit brings down strongholds in my mind.

You have given me your GOSPEL as covering for my feet.

Your gospel on my tongue takes me places where I can glorify you.

Your Refuge Is Safe

Have mercy on me, my God, have mercy on me, for in you I take refuge. I will take refuge in the shadow of your wings until the disaster has passed.

Psalm 57:1

Blessed is the one who perseveres under trial because, having stood the test, that person will receive the crown of life that the Lord has promised to those who love him.

James 1:12

Thank You For Refuge

You are my tower of strength.

You are my strong fortress.

You are my solid rock.

You give me refuge from the adversary.

You help me when I am confounded.

You give me grace that is sufficient to bear the trial.

You give me comfort amid affliction.

You provide me a way of escape.

You alert me of ways that are not constructive.

You refine me as gold.

You develop in me the fruit of the Spirit.

You cause my faith to mature.

You help me to stand firm.

You fill my heart with courage.

You help me bring glory and honor to your Name.

You are my REFUGE!

Praise Notes

Thank You for Help

You Are My Helper

God is our Father no matter in what circumstance we find ourselves today. He is the defender of the fatherless and the widow. He takes care of the orphan, the poor, and the needy. Jesus says in Matthew 10:29 that even a tiny sparrow does not fall to the ground without the Father's care.

Our Father is a shelter from the storm, a stronghold in the time of trouble, and a refuge from the attack of the evil one. He is faithful to us even when we are not faithful to Him.

He hears our cry for help and comes to our rescue quickly. He answers all our prayers according to His will. He knows what is best for us because He formed us in our mother's womb. He calls us by name and loves us unconditionally.

He does not give us according to what our deeds deserve because He is merciful, but loads us with benefits that we do not deserve because He is gracious. He is committed to helping us to our very end. There is no one like our God.

He is our loving FATHER!

Your Help Is Ever Present

God is our refuge and strength, an ever-present help in trouble.

Psalm 46:1

My help comes from the LORD, the Maker of heaven and earth. He will not let your foot slip – he who watches over you will not slumber;

Psalm 121:2-3

Thank You For Help

You are the defender of the fatherless.

You are the rescuer of the devastated.

You are the savior of the rejected.

You are the lifter of the cast down.

You are the guardian of the poor.

You are the provider of the needy.

You are the strength of the weak.

You are the redeemer of the deserted.

You are the help of the helpless.

You are the caretaker of the abandoned.

You are the hope of the forsaken.

You are the restorer of the broken.

You are the healer of the wounded.

You are the lover of my soul.

You are my ever-present help.

You are my HELPER!

You Are My Comfort

Thank You for Comfort

Your Comfort Is Uplifting

The LORD Almighty says in Isaiah 51:12

"I, even I, am he who **comforts** you. Who are you that you fear mere mortals, human beings who are but grass."

Thank You For Comfort

You hear my weeping and notice my tears.

Your Holy Spirit is my comforter.

Your Shepherd's rod and staff are my comfort.

Your goodness and kindness are my comfort.

Your tender mercies are my comfort.

Your unfailing love is my comfort.

Your word brings me comfort and relief.

You comfort me as a mother comforts her child.

Your promises preserve my life.

You comfort me in my painful toil.

You comfort me in my suffering.

You have compassion on me when I am afflicted.

You help me with loss and disappointment.

You comfort me when I my heart faints within me.

You console me when I am stricken with grief.

You see my cares and take it into your hand.

Your Compassion Is Unfailing

Shout for joy, you heavens; rejoice, you earth; burst into song, you mountains! For the LORD **comforts** his people and will have compassion on his afflicted ones.

Isaiah 49:13

A bruised reed he will not break, and a smoldering wick he will not snuff out. In faithfulness he will bring forth justice;

Isaiah 42:3

Thank You For Comfort

You remove obstacles out of my way.

You sympathize with me in my weakness.

You don't ever give up on me.

You do not let my hope perish.

You hear my voice in the morning.

You hold me by your powerful hand.

You lift me up and help me stand.

You relieve me from my anxieties.

You remember me with great love.

You remove my sorrow and sighing.

You replace the heaviness in my heart with your praise.

You trade beauty for my brokenness.

You turn my mourning into dancing.

You faithfully answer my prayers.

You surround me with your favor.

You work out all things for my good.

Your Kindness Is Consoling

The LORD, the LORD, the compassionate and gracious God, slow to anger, abounding in love and faithfulness.

Exodus 34:6

You gave me life and showed me kindness, and in your providence watched over my spirit.

Job 10:12

Thank You For Comfort

You comfort births thanksgiving in my heart.

Your comfort puts songs on my lips.

Your loving-kindness is more than life to me.

Your mercies are new every morning.

You fill my soul with joy and gladness.

You are the God of all comfort.

You are the Father of compassion.

You are my COMFORTER!

You Are My Healer

Thank You for Healing

Your Healing Is Precious

"He himself bore our sins" in his body on the cross, so that we might die to sins and live for righteousness; "by his wounds you have been healed."

1 Peter 2:24

Thank You For Healing

Jesus, you are the Miracle Worker!

You fed the five thousand with five loaves of bread.

You walked on the water and brought the storm to calm.

You opened blind eyes with a touch of your hand.

You made the deaf to hear and the mute to speak.

You cleansed the leper and caused the lame to walk.

You raised the widow's son, and Lazarus from the dead.

Your cured the incurable and made them whole.

You healed all who were under the power of the devil.

Jesus by your stripes you have purchased my healing.

Your body was broken to make my body whole.

You took all my weaknesses and bore all my sicknesses.

Your gracious Word brings healing to my bones.

Your precious blood cleanses my body.

You fill me with strength as I wait on you.

You hold me up with your righteous right hand.

Your Healing is Priceless

LORD God Almighty says in Exodus 15:26b

"I am the LORD, who heals you."

Worship the LORD your God, and his blessing will be on your food and water. I will take away sickness from among you.

Exodus 23:25

Thank You For Healing

Your power brings healing to my body.

You bring health and wholeness to my mind.

You rescue my body from wasting away in grief.

You rescue me from the grave so I can fulfill your purpose.

You fill me with power when I am tired and worn out.

You heal me so I can do your will and bring you glory.

Your mercy brings health and restoration.

You restore my health to a vigorous life.

Your Spirit refreshes my soul.

Your Spirit renews my mind.

Your Spirit gives me a keen and sound mind.

You send your word and heal my diseases.

You shield my life from deadly diseases.

You restore my health and heal my wounds.

You protect my bones and give them strength.

You heal my emotions and make me strong.

Your Pardon Is Invaluable

Praise the LORD, my soul, and forget not all his benefits – who forgives all your sins and heals all your diseases,

Psalm 103:2-3

He sent out his word and healed them; he rescued them from the grave.

Psalm 107:20

Thank You For Healing

Your presence brings health and nourishment to my body.

You make my heart glad and tongue to rejoice.

You give me life and length of days.

You are the Sun of Righteousness rising with healing in its rays.

You are my HEALER!

Praise Notes

Thank You for Purpose

You Are My Maker

Our Creator has meticulously planned how and for what purpose he brings us to this earth. He selected our parents, the place and time of our birth, the color of our hair, and every detail about us, so we can fulfill his divine purpose.

Not only does God have a unique purpose for us, but also a wonderful plan of how we can fulfill that divine purpose. He created us in our mother's womb and knows what is best for us. He reveals his plans to us through the Holy Spirit. The Holy Spirit guides us and empowers us to do God's will.

God's plan for our lives is for us to know Him and to make Him known. It does not matter what our vocation. God has good works for us to do in every situation. He wants to manifest his love, his goodness, and his wisdom through his children. God can be glorified through our lives in all places, at all times, and in all seasons.

When we live by the Master's plan we will have abundant life – a life filled with purpose, love, joy, and peace that the world cannot give or take away.

Your Plan Is Prosperous

For I know the plans I have for you, "declares the LORD, "plans to prosper you and not to harm you, plans to give you hope and a future.

Jeremiah 29:11

Thank You For Purpose

You formed man out of the dust of the earth.

You breathed into man your breath of life.

You formed me in my mother's womb.

You created me for your purpose.

You have called me by name.

You have a marvelous plan for my life.

Your plan for my life is to prosper me.

Your plan for my life gives me a future.

Your plan for my life gives me hope.

You know when I sit down and when I arise.

You know my thoughts before I speak them out.

You have determined the days of my existence on earth.

You are with me if I go to the deepest depth a man can reach.

You are with me if I go to the highest height a man can reach.

You see me always whether I am in the light or in the dark.

Your thoughts over me are more than the number of the sand.

Your Thoughts Are Immense

How precious to me are your thoughts, God!
How vast is the sum of them!

Psalm 139:17

Thank You For Purpose

Your thoughts over me are precious to me.

You have set me apart from birth.

You reveal the mystery of your purpose to me.

You equip me to fulfill your purpose.

You open doors for me that no one can shut.

You help me gain knowledge and understanding.

You give me insight and intelligence.

You give me wisdom and tact of speech.

You fill my future with new opportunities.

You enable me to do good deeds.

You bestow abundant provision of grace on me.

You keep my lamp burning for your glory.

You catch me when I fall as I walk with you.

You give me the ability to make right decisions.

You help me know the hope of your calling in my life.

You know what is going to happen in the future.

Your Purpose Is Firm

I am the LORD your God, who teaches you what is best for you, who directs you in the way you should go.

Isaiah 48:17b

Thank You For Purpose

You fill me with the knowledge of your will.

You bring to focus the vision for my future.

You enable me to do good works that bring you glory.

You help me fulfill the purpose you have for me.

You are the author and finisher of my faith.

You hold the seasons of my life in your precious hands.

You will not allow the evil one to destroy my destiny.

You are faithful to complete the good work you started in me.

You are my POTTER – I am the clay.

You Are My Guide

Thank You for Guidance

Your Instruction Is Trustworthy

He guides the humble in what is right and teaches them his way.

Psalm 25:9

I will instruct you and teach you in the way you should go; I will guide you with My eye.

Psalm 32:8

New King James Version (NKJV)

Thank You For Guidance

You guide me by your Holy Spirit.

You guide me by your Word.

You guide me by your mighty hand.

You guide me along the right path.

You lead me in the paths of righteousness.

You instruct me in the way I should go.

You lead me in the way everlasting.

You guide me along the path of peace.

You help me keep moving forward.

You make level the rough ways.

You lead me in a straight path.

Your Word is a lamp that lights my way.

Your Word is a light that informs my decisions.

Your Word is living and is actively teaching me.

Your Word judges my thoughts and attitudes.

Your Word rebukes and corrects me.

Your Path Is Right

He refreshes my soul. He guides me along the right paths for his name's sake.

Psalm 23:3

But when he, the Spirit of truth, comes, he will guide you into all the truth. He will not speak on his own; he will speak only what he hears, and he will tell you what is yet to come.

John 16:13

Thank You For Guidance

You guide me in your truth.

You guide me when I humble myself.

You put your laws in my mind.

You write your laws on my heart.

You renew my mind in the knowledge of my Creator.

You turn the darkness in my path into light.

You guide me away from the influences that would mislead me.

You direct my heart to your goodness, mercy, and love.

You guide me along the unversed path.

You guide me so my works would not be in vain.

You guide me to friends who love and serve You.

You bring godly mentors along my path.

You help me see the possibilities that are not obvious.

You order my steps to conform to your will.

You guide me according to the plan you have for my life.

You lead me to the springs of living water.

Your Guidance is Enduring

For this God is our God for ever and ever; he will be our guide even to the end.

Psalm 48:14

Thank You For Guidance

You guide me because of your great name.

You guide me by your counsel.

You guide me by your wisdom.

You guide me to your desired outcome.

You will guide me unto the end.

You are my GUIDE!

You Are My Life

Thank You For Abundant Life

Your Life In Me Is Fulfilling

The thief comes only to steal and kill and destroy; I have come that they may have life, and have it to the full.

John 10:10

Thank You For Abundant Life

You pour out your Spirit upon me.

You forgive my sins and any bad intention of my heart.

You incline my heart to walk obediently to your word.

You give me strength to withstand the desires of the flesh.

You reveal the depth of your love and grace to me.

You purify my heart and make me holy.

You guard the precious truth of the gospel in me.

You help me overcome temptations.

You help me know you better every day.

You help me live wisely.

You help me be truthful.

You build me up to reflect your kindness.

You put the fear of God in my heart.

You fill my heart with your presence.

You let your word flourish in my heart.

You let the fruit of righteousness manifest in my life.

Your Righteousness Reigns

For if, by the trespass of the one man, death reigned through that one man, how much more will those who receive God's abundant provision of grace and of the gift of righteousness reign in life through the one man, Jesus Christ!

Romans 5:17

Thank You For Abundant Life

You help me forget the past and look to the future with hope.

You shine the light of your truth in me.

You discipline me in love.

You make me strong and steadfast in faith.

You empower me for works done by faith.

You sharpen my vision like that of an eagle.

You give me the power to love and to forgive.

You help me to be rooted and grounded in love.

You give me revelation from heaven.

You give me discernment.

You give me understanding.

You give me sound judgement.

You increase my faith.

You reveal the mystery of the Gospel to me.

You train my hands for works that will defeat the enemy.

You help me put off my sinful nature.

Your Blessing is Abundant

And God is able to bless you abundantly, so that in all things at all times, having all that you need, you will abound in every good work.

2 Corinthians 9:8

Thank You For Abundant Life

You give me strength to overcome the troubles.

You help me think clearly and make good choices.

You fill my heart with love for people around me.

You fill my heart with love for my enemies.

You help me see what you see in others.

You ignite my heart with passion for the lost around me.

You enable me to speak your word with boldness.

You help me be your spokesperson.

You help me represent Jesus in a relevant way.

You help me bring joy to the hearts of others.

You help me bring healing and comfort to others.

You help me be sensible with my words

You help me serve you wholeheartedly.

You work in me to do all that is pleasing to you.

You count me worthy of your calling.

You help me be steadfast in prayer.

Your Love Is Unending

Surely your goodness and love will follow me all the days of my life, and I will dwell in the house of the LORD forever.

Psalm 23:6

Thank You For Abundant Life

You extend my reach and influence.

You make me the head and not the tail.

You reward me for prayers done in secret.

You help me be fervent in spirit serving you.

You fill me with confident hope.

You show me the wonders of your love.

You guard my mind with peace.

You give rest to my soul.

You put songs of joy in my heart.

You cause me to be victorious in Christ Jesus.

You give me the desires of my heart that conform to your will.

You do immeasurably more than I can ask or imagine.

You crown me with your lovingkindness.

You carry me in your everlasting arms.

You satisfy me with the joy of your presence.

You are my LIFE!

You Are My Reward

Thank You for Rewards

We come with nothing into this world and will leave with nothing, as well. But **everything we do here on earth counts** for something. According to the scriptures, Jesus is coming back to take us home, with rewards for all the work we have done on earth.

What we do with our life and how we do it demonstrates what and whom we believe. If Jesus is our Savior and Lord, we know where we will spend our eternity. However, what we believe and obey determines how we will spend eternity. If the reward that Jesus brings for us makes no difference in heaven, then we would not need them at all. Since they are given to us after we leave this earth, I believe they are going to make a difference in how we experience heaven.

The reward we will receive is not based on how well we do when compared to someone else, but it is according to what we do, and how we do it with what we are given. God has a unique blueprint for each of our lives. He has predetermined the good works that we must do to bring Him glory.

"For we are God's handiwork, created in Christ Jesus to do good works, which God prepared in advance for us to do."

Ephesians 2:10.

Paul writes in 2 Corinthians 2:14b, *"and uses us to spread the aroma of the knowledge of him everywhere"*.

God has made it possible for us to know His plans and to do those good works through the Holy Spirit that dwells in us. Our mission is to live out God's love, grace, and truth, wherever we are and in whatever we do.

Nothing on earth – neither devil, nor sickness, nor defeat – can hinder our destiny when we are fully engaged in following the direction of the Holy Spirit and doing God's will in our lives. Jesus has purchased healing for our body, soul, and mind. He will deliver us from the evil one and guide us on our journey.

When we live FOR God today, we will not only experience the abundant life on this earth while we fulfill His mission, but also be richly and righteously rewarded in eternity.

Your Reward Is Righteous

Commit your way to the LORD; trust in him and he will do this: He will make your righteous reward shine like the dawn, your vindication like the noonday sun.

Psalm 37:5-6

For the Son of Man is going to come in his Father's glory with his angels, and then he will reward each person according to what they have done.

Matthew 10:42

Thank You For Rewards

You have an indestructible inheritance for me as my reward.

You reward me for keeping your Word.

You reward me for honoring your commands.

You reward me for seeking your righteousness.

You reward me for pursuing peace.

You reward me for all the good deeds I do.

You reward me for serving wholeheartedly.

You reward me for being kind to the poor.

You reward me for giving cheerfully.

You reward me for serving voluntarily without recompense.

Your reward me for everything I do in your name.

You reward those who suffer for your name's sake.

You will give a crown as reward for running the race with patience.

You will give a crown of life as reward for enduring temptation.

You will give a victor's crown as reward for being faithful.

You will give the hidden manna as reward to the victorious.

Your Reward is Lasting

Look I am coming soon! My reward is with me, and I will give to each person according to what they have done.

Revelation 22:12

Thank You For Rewards

You will give the crown of glory to those who willingly shepherd the flock who are under their care.

You will give the morning star as a reward to the one who does your will to the end.

You will give a crown of righteousness as reward to those who long for your appearance and finish the race well.

Your reward is just.

Your reward is rich.

Your reward is sure.

Your reward is righteous.

Your reward is a lasting possession.

You will reward me when you come with your angels.

Your eternal presence is my greatest reward.

Your unceasing fellowship is my glorious reward.

Jesus you took the crown of thorns to adorn me with the crown of life.

YOU are my exceeding great REWARD!

You Are My Future

Thank You For Heaven

Your Mansion Is Magnificent

My Father's house has many rooms; if that were not so, would I have told you that I am going to prepare a place for you? And if I go and prepare a place for you, I will come back and take you to be with me that you also may be where I am.

John 14:2-3

THANK YOU FOR HEAVEN

You have called me to live with you in your eternal glory.

You are preparing a new heaven and a new earth for me.

You are the architect and builder of the new city where I will live forever.

Your power will transform my mortal body to a glorious body.

You have prepared the heavenly country I can call my own.

You have provided me a heavenly inheritance that can never perish, spoil, or fade.

You will come in the clouds with trumpet sounds to take me home.

You will bring me to my loved ones who have gone before.

You will wipe every tear from my eyes.

Your glorious appearing is my blessed hope.

You will make all things new again for old things are no more.

You will give me a new name.

You will bring me to the "Tree of Life" once again.

You will lead me to the pure Water of Life that is as clear as a crystal.

Your Coming Will Be Glorious

For the Lord himself will come down from heaven, with a loud command, with the voice of the archangel and with the trumpet call of God, and the dead in Christ will rise first.

1 Thessalonians 4:16-17

Thank You For Heaven

You will bring me into the joyful assembly of thousands and thousands of angels.

You will set me in a kingdom that will never be destroyed.

You will fill me with boundless peace and crown me with everlasting joy.

You are my FUTURE!

Praise Notes

Section 5

Commitment

And forgive us our debts, as we also, have forgiven our debtors

Matthew 6:13

A true mark of God's righteousness in our life is forgiving people who hurt us.

A high priest in the Old Testament never sat in the temple or in the tabernacle of worship. We read in Hebrews 8, that Jesus our Great High Priest, having offered himself as a sacrifice on the cross for our sanctification once and for all, entered the true tabernacle of God in heaven with his own precious blood and **sat down** at the right hand of the Father, His Majesty.

However, as Stephen was stoned to death for witnessing about Jesus as the Messiah, we read, in Acts 7:56b, "I see heaven open and the **Son of Man standing** at the right hand of God.", and in Acts 7:60, "Lord do not hold this sin against them."

I can only imagine from these verses that when Stephen fell dead, cast off his earthly robe (his mortal body), and entered the courts of heaven, that Jesus **stood up** to honor and receive Stephen's spirit. I think it is because, in Stephen, Jesus saw himself on the cross crying out while in agony, "Father forgive them for they do not know what they are doing" (Luke 24:47). Jesus saw his imprint on Stephen who as he was dying forgave those who were stoning him to death.

We are more like Jesus when we forgive those who hurt us.

I Forgive

Forgive, and you will be forgiven.

Luke 6:37b

But if you do not forgive others their sins, your Father will not forgive your sins.

Matthew 6:15

And when you stand praying, if you hold anything against anyone, forgive them, so that your Father in heaven may forgive you your sins.

Mark 11:25

I Forgive

Lord help me forgive.

Lord I forgive my father ____________________.

Lord I forgive my mother ____________________.

Lord I forgive my husband ____________________.

Lord I forgive my wife ____________________.

Lord I forgive my brother ____________________.

Lord I forgive my sister ____________________.

Lord I forgive my uncle ____________________.

Lord I forgive my aunt ____________________.

Lord I forgive my son ____________________.

Lord I forgive my daughter ____________________.

Lord I forgive my grandson ____________________.

Lord I forgive my granddaughter ____________________.

Lord I forgive my grandfather ____________________.

Lord I forgive my grandmother ____________________.

Lord I forgive my cousin ____________________.

Praise Notes

I Forgive

Lord I forgive my nephew ________________.

Lord I forgive my niece ________________.

Lord I forgive my relative ________________.

Lord I forgive my school teacher ________________.

Lord I forgive my friend ________________.

Lord I forgive my coworker ________________.

Lord I forgive my neighbor ________________.

Lord I forgive my brother in Christ ________________.

Lord I forgive my sister in Christ ________________.

Lord I forgive my leader ________________.

Lord I forgive my mentor ________________.

Lord I forgive everyone who has hurt me in the past.

For if you forgive other people when they sin against you,

your heavenly Father will also forgive you.

– Matthew 6:14

I Surrender

There is a place of peace, power, and purpose in this world – and it begins with one word, *Surrender.*

Joni Lamb, Surrender All (Colorado: Waterbrook Press, 2011)

I COMMIT

I will worship you.

I will adore you.

I will praise you.

I will sing of you.

I will love you.

I will come before you.

I will lift my hands to you.

I will bow down to you.

I will seek your face.

I will listen to you.

I will wait on you.

I will follow you.

I will trust in you.

I will obey you.

I will honor you.

I will serve you.

I Commit

But you, God, see the trouble of the afflicted; you consider their grief and take it in hand. The victims **commit** themselves to you; you are the helper of the fatherless.

Psalm 10:14

I Commit

I will cry out to you.

I will pour out my heart to you.

I will incline my ear to you.

I will raise my eyes to you.

I will look to you for help.

I will rely on you.

I will learn more of you.

I will believe in you.

I will tell of your love.

I will proclaim your goodness.

I will speak of your majesty.

I will tell of your mighty works.

I will bring my tithes to your house.

I will worship you with my offerings.

I will kneel in your awesome presence.

I will prostrate before your throne.

I Rejoice

Let us rejoice and be glad and give him glory! For the wedding of the Lamb has come, and his bride has made herself ready.

Revelation 19:7

I COMMIT

I will rejoice in you.

I will bless you.

I will exalt you.

I will say you are my God.

I will say you are my Father.

I will say you are my Lord.

I will say you are my King.

I will live FOR you today.

I will live WITH you forever!

Amen

"Amen! Praise and glory and wisdom and thanks and honor and power and strength be to our God forever and ever. Amen!"

Revelation 7:12

Concluding Thought

God so loved the world that he gave his Son Jesus to pay the penalty for our sins. By acknowledging Jesus Christ as our Lord and Savior, and asking him to forgive our sins, we receive the gift of eternal life. Then when we die and our mortal bodies return to the earth from which they were formed, our spirits born again in Christ Jesus will go back to God. Finally, we will be clothed again with an immortal resurrected body, and live with God forever and ever.

If Jesus is not your Savior and Lord, this awesome God whom you have been reading about, longs for you to know him.

A Simple Prayer

Lord Jesus, I believe you are the Son of God and you died for me. I ask you to forgive my sins. I receive the gift of eternal life that you have offered through your death on the cross. I thank you for forgiving all my sins.

Father God, I thank you for Jesus Christ. I thank you for the Holy Spirit. Fill me with your Holy Spirit to guide me, and to help me do your will. I want to fulfill your purpose for my life. I ask this in Jesus name. Amen.

Know God has a great plan for your life. You are created for his purpose. The Holy Spirit lives inside of you to guide you and empower you to do his will. As you obey the promptings of the Holy Spirt, pursue righteousness, faith, love and peace, you will experience the abundant life Jesus died to give you.

Your best life is ahead!

I pray for God's love and peace to be poured into your heart in great measure as you declare his praises every day.

Praise Notes

About the Author

The author grew up in a five-generation missionary family, dedicated to spreading the gospel around the world. She draws on her experience of planting churches, pioneering a Christian school, ministering in songwriting and teaching God's word, raising two now adult children, living in multiple continents, and eventually working in corporate America, to bless others with what she has learned and experienced with the help of the Holy Spirit.

Praise Notes

Notes

The excellent resource that helped me write this book is www.biblegateway.com.

I am grateful for the ability to search through the scriptures swiftly and effectively.